Cousins
Morgan Brody
My Family
EZ
READERS

Creating Young Nonfiction Readers

EZ Readers lets children delve into nonfiction at beginning reading levels. Young readers are introduced to new concepts, facts, ideas, and vocabulary.

Tips for Reading Nonfiction with Beginning Readers

Talk about Nonfiction

Begin by explaining that nonfiction books give us information that is true. The book will be organized around a specific topic or idea, and we may learn new facts through reading.

Look at the Parts

Most nonfiction books have helpful features. Our *EZ Readers* include a Contents page, an index, a picture glossary, and color photographs. Share the purpose of these features with your reader.

Contents

Located at the front of a book, the Contents displays a list of the big ideas within the book and where to find them.

Index

An index is an alphabetical list of topics and the page numbers where they are found.

Picture Glossary

Located at the back of the book, a picture glossary contains key words/phrases that are related to the topic.

Photos/Charts

A lot of information can be found by "reading" the charts and photos found within nonfiction text. Help your reader learn more about the different ways information can be displayed.

With a little help and guidance about reading nonfiction, you can feel good about introducing a young reader to the world of *EZ Readers* nonfiction books.

Printing 1 2 3 4 5 6 7 8 9

Author: Morgan Brody
Designer: Ed Morgan
Editor: Sharon F. Dorasamy

Names/credits:
Title: Cousins / by Morgan Brody
Description: Hallandale, FL :
Mitchell Lane Publishers, [2018]

Series: My Family

Library bound ISBN: 9781680202311

eBook ISBN: 9781680202328

EZ readers is an imprint of
Mitchell Lane Publishers

Photo credits: Getty Images, Freepik.com

Contents

I love my cousins.

We go to school together.

BRAZIL

We go on
vacation together.

We take pictures together.

We go to birthday parties together.

We love to play **games.**

We love **sleepovers.**

We love our **family.**

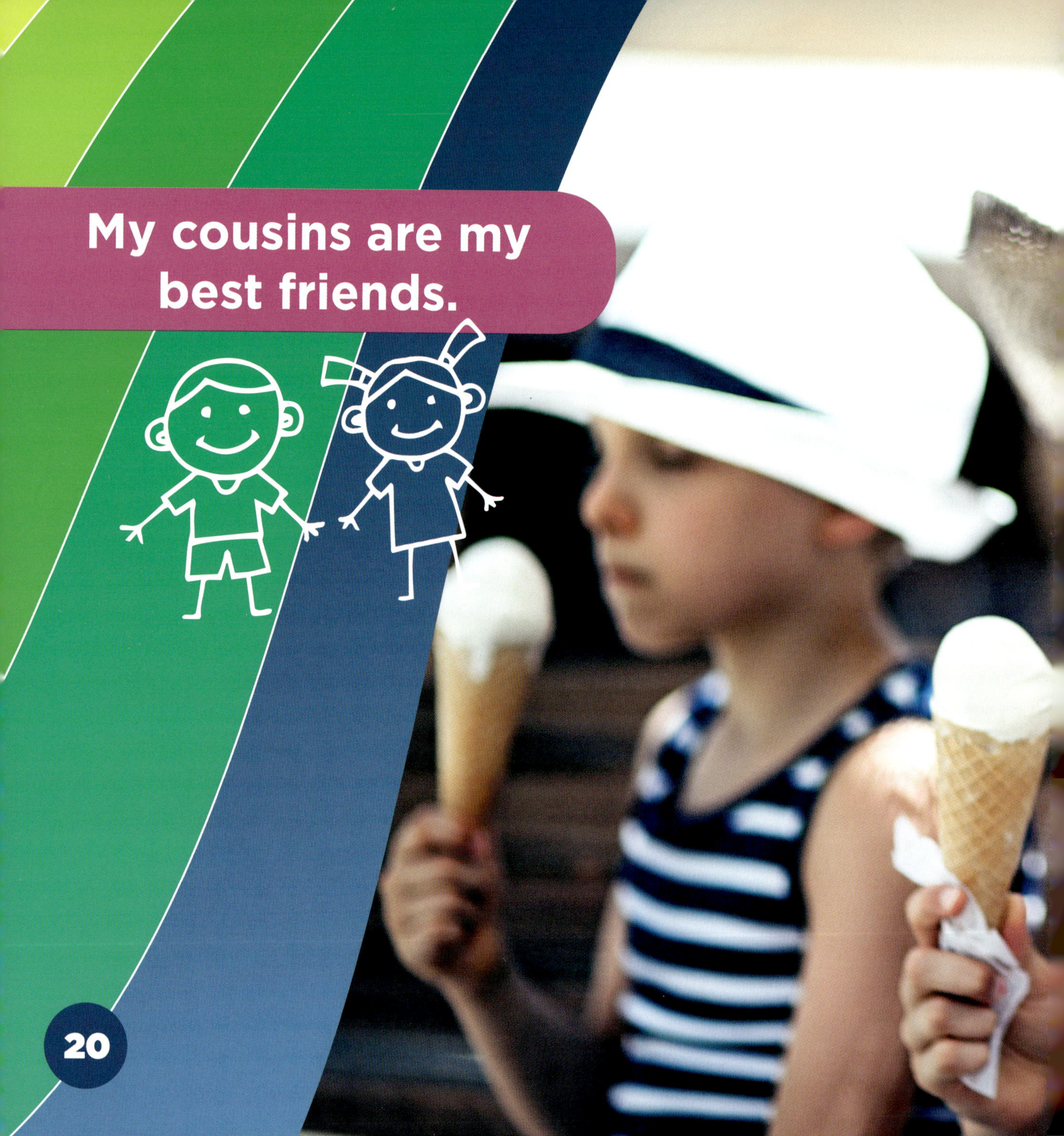

My cousins are my best friends.

Picture Glossary

family
A group of people related to each other

parties
A social event in which entertainment, food, and drinks are provided

games
A physical or mental activity or contest that has rules that people do for fun

pictures
Something that shows what a person looks like

school
A place where students go to learn

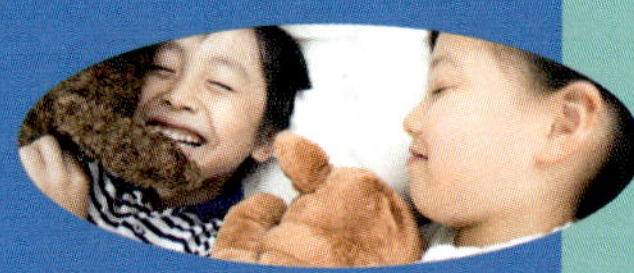

sleepovers
A party where one or more children stay overnight at one person's house

vacation
Time spent away from home, school, or work in order to have fun

Do your cousins have nicknames?

What do you and your cousins like to do the most?

What kinds of things do your older cousins teach you?

What things do you teach your younger cousins?

Do you have a favorite cousin? Explain why.

Index